W9-AVA-007

YOU PARENTED YOUR CHILD

FOR APPROXIMATELY

936 WEEKS FROM

THE DAY THEY WERE BORN

UNTIL NOW.

WELCOME TO WEEK 937

AND BEYOND.

—

"TEACH US TO NUMBER OUR DAYS
(OR MAYBE WEEKS)
THAT WE MAY GAIN A HEART OF WISDOM."

PSALM 90:12

18 PLUS
PARENTING YOUR EMERGING ADULT

www.JustAPhase.com
Published by Orange, a division of The reThink Group, Inc.,
5870 Charlotte Lane, Suite 300,
Cumming, GA 30040 U.S.A.

©2018 The Phase Project
Authors: Steven Argue and Kara Powell
Editing Team: Crystal Chiang, Karen Wilson, Steve Argue, and Mike Jeffries
Project Manager: Nate Brandt

Art Direction: Ryan Boon and Hannah Crosby
Book Design: Jacob Hunt and Sharon van Rossum

Phase Concept: Kristen Ivy and Reggie Joiner

Printed in the United States of America
First Edition
2 3 4 5 6 7 8 9 10 11

05/30/18

18 PLUS

PARENTING YOUR EMERGING ADULT

STEVEN ARGUE - KARA POWELL

TABLE OF CONTENTS

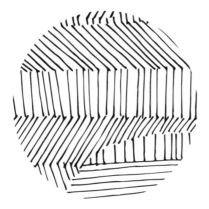

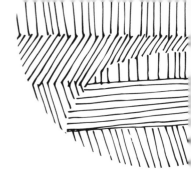

EVERY PHASE IS A

TIMEFRAME

IN A PERSON'S LIFE

WHEN YOU CAN

LEVERAGE

DISTINCTIVE

OPPORTUNITIES

TO INFLUENCE

THEIR

future.

18 PLUS

—

THE PHASE WHEN
YOUR EMERGING
ADULT PULLS AWAY
MORE, NEEDS YOU
AGAIN, DOES THINGS
FOR THE FIRST TIME
AND YOU BOTH
KEEP ASKING,

"What now?"

THIS IS THE YEAR YOU HAVE IMAGINED FOR EIGHTEEN YEARS

You may be surprised how loud the emptiness sounds when someone so familiar in your world suddenly disappears. Of course, you may also rediscover a little personal freedom of your own. What do you mean there's no game to attend, no form to sign, no forgotten books to take to the school at the last minute? And how did the milk not get consumed before it expired?

THEY MAY COST YOU MORE EVEN THOUGH YOU SEE THEM LESS

Even if they aren't physically present, their presence may still be felt—especially in your bank account. Whether you are helping fund their continued education or making a deposit for their first apartment, there's a good chance you haven't stopped paying for some expenses in their world. They may also cost you some unpredictable time as well. You never know when they may call looking for advice, affirmation, or maybe just a reminder of home.

GIVE ADVICE WHEN THEY ASK FOR IT

The good news is that every 18 and 19-year-old knows what they want and has a precise plan for their life. Wait? That's not true? They might amaze you with all they can do on their own, but there's also still a lot left to figure out. Where will they live? Will they get married? What kind of work will ultimately bring them fulfillment? They want your advice, but only in small doses, and only when they ask for it. This is a season to re-engage your child in a new way, not as a parent but more as a peer as you transition your relationship for the future.

Today's emerging adults face a world that is more complicated, more competitive, requires more preparation, and offers more options. What your son or daughter is navigating—and the support they need from you along the way—is likely different than you think. No matter what television and movies suggest, now is *not* the time to shift to "autopilot parenting." It's more like ready-at-any-moment's-notice parenting. You never know when they may call (or, okay, text) looking for advice on how to fix . . .

A car

A failing grade

An overdrawn checking account

A sticky work situation

A broken heart

And in those moments? They'll need you.
In other moments, they'll need affirmation, encouragement, someone to believe in them, or a reminder of home. Sometimes they'll tell you what they need. Other times, you'll have to figure it out on your own. Either way, parenting isn't over. Not by a long shot. You've just entered a new phase. Parenting will look a lot different now. And just like when . . .

your two-year-old turned three

your fifth grader became a sixth grader

your middle schooler started high school . . .

the most important thing is that you still show up.

18 PLUS
THE BEST PHASE

EMERGING ADULTHOOD IS THE BEST PHASE

This is the moment when your 936-week investment begins to pay off as you watch your teenager emerge as a young adult. Chances are your kid is making some of their first post-high-school choices. Maybe they're pursuing a degree. Maybe they've landed a full-time job. Maybe they've joined the military. But no matter if they're moving out of the house or into your basement, your kid is now more responsible for their friendships, romantic interests, careers, and spirituality than ever before. And because of your guidance and support, they're (mostly) ready for it! This season of parenting can be both exciting and hopeful as you watch your son or daughter make decisions that will set the trajectory of their future.[1]

SO WHAT EXACTLY IS "EMERGING"?

Your kid probably doesn't think of themselves as "emerging." They may try to convince you (and themselves) that they've got this, or that they're ready. (So you've heard. A few times.) Yet, they'll also admit that stepping out on their own is scary, uncertain, and ill-defined. They may be clear on who they're not anymore but still grappling with who they are becoming. That's why we use the word "emerging" to describe this specific phase of your kid's life. It's an in-between season. High school is in the rearview mirror. Major milestones of adulthood—like marriage, family, and career—are still on the horizon. So even though your kid is legally considered an adult, you know (and they really know) they aren't quite finished growing and don't have it all figured out yet.

In other words, they still need you.

YOU'VE BEEN HERE BEFORE, BUT THIS FEELS (AND IS) DIFFERENT

The truth is, this isn't the first time your kid has "emerged" as someone new. New phases tend to cause a double-whammy for parents: We measure our kid's progress so far, while amplifying our own anxieties about this new, unexplored season. So during a time of change, we may attempt to "help" in two ways. First, we try to take control to ensure that our kids (and we) make it through the transition. But continually taking control has diminishing returns over the course of your kid's life. What worked when they were in preschool doesn't, of course, work when they're 13. Now that they're on the verge of adulthood, your attempts at control will almost always land flat.

The second way we "help" is by assuming that their post-high school transition will look just like ours did. The reality is that it will be strikingly different.

We know your kid's world may seem familiar to you.
Because you remember what it's like to be their age, right?
(And it wasn't that long ago, right? Right?)
But the world they live in is hugely different from the world you and I experienced as graduates.

This unique, dynamic phase will help us discover a new closeness with our emerging adults, challenge our dreams for them, and confront our own insecurities—as well as stretch our worldviews.

However, some things won't change.
They'll probably still need some money.

EVERY EMERGING ADULT IS UNIQUE

Some move away.
Some don't.

Some want to start a business.
Some want to throw a party.

Some have a clear plan now.
Some have big dreams and no idea about
how to get there.

Some are still dating a high school sweetheart.
Some are dating someone new every weekend.

Some live alone.
Some live with roommates.
Some live with you.

Some have all the answers.
Some have all the questions.

Some have a few close friends.
Some have thousands of social media followers.
Some have both.
Some believe everything they did five years ago.
Some question everything they believed five years ago.
Some find something new to question every five minutes.

And even though every young adult is unique, they all have
some traits in common. This book is designed to help you
make the most of the challenges and opportunities that
come with parenting an emerging adult.

Remember: We haven't met YOUR emerging adult.
This book is just about a lot of emerging adults.

FOR SOME EIGHTEEN+ SOUNDS LIKE . . .

THINGS THEY MIGHT SAY

I'm thinking about taking a year off.

Why does everyone keep asking me what I want to do with my life?

I don't know if I'll ever get married.

No matter how much I do, I still feel behind.

I'm not like you.

I don't believe that anymore.

Don't treat me like I'm in high school.

I have a question.

You want me to *pay rent*?

I'm not going to be home for the holiday.

I'm thinking about a different major.

I'm working on my personal brand.

Why does college cost so much money?

I'll pay you back.

Text me!

Um, could you please not comment on my posts?

THINGS YOU MIGHT SAY

How long will you be home?

When will you be home?

It'll be okay.

What do you mean you don't want a "normal" job?

What's a start-up?

Why didn't you reply to my text?

What do you mean you can sign your own release form?

I thought by now you would stop asking me for money.

I thought by now you would stop playing video games.

I'm not sure I believe that anymore, either.

When I was your age . . .

I have a question.

I miss you.

I'm worried about you.

I'm proud of you.

Did you see my post on Facebook?

Call me!

UNDERSTAND THE PHASE

—

THE SIX WAYS YOUR EMERGING ADULT IS CHANGING

NEWSFLASH:

Even though your kid is no longer in high school, 936 weeks after they were born, you're still parenting.

Maybe this reality makes you happy.

Or maybe it makes you feel exhausted. Aren't you supposed to graduate parenting when they graduate from high school?

Well, no. Because the truth is this: parenting doesn't have a finish line. Each new phase is just a corner that takes you into a new phase of parenting.

And this phase? Well, you now have some un-parenting to do.

This doesn't mean that your parenting has been bad. You did a great job during third grade. Sixth grade? Crushed it. You even parented gracefully through the twists and turns of tenth grade (although maybe there were moments when you were ready to give up on parenting altogether).

But now they're in a new phase. And your parenting is, too.

In other words, the parenting that got you here won't get you there.

So you'll need to pay attention to your kid.
And to yourself.
Because this journey toward adulthood isn't just about them.
It will challenge and shape you in new ways, too.

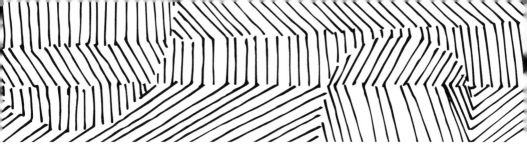

During each phase of your child's life, they change in six different ways. As you begin your journey with your emerging adult in these six areas, your role will become less authoritative and more relational.

You'll be less of a commander, and more of a companion. And before it's over, maybe even a friend.

one

WHAT'S CHANGING CULTURALLY

THE QUARTERLIFE CRISIS

Parents of emerging adults often face their own midlife crisis.

While your potential midlife crisis is a topic for another book, your emerging adult child is in a parallel process some refer to as the "quarterlife crisis."[2] Think of it as a mid-midlife crisis, but earlier and without the new sports car.

While previous generations have faced important questions in their journeys after high school, the road map for today's young people is more complicated. Way more. Your child likely has more opportunities, and more possible routes to take, than ever before. They can go almost anywhere—physically or virtually. They can become anything or anyone they want. It's possible for them to not only *choose* a career path but to create an entirely *new* path.

Many of these options will require education, which may be why the number of students attending colleges and universities has increased in recent years.[3] In fact, two-thirds of high school graduates attend college, a higher proportion than ever before in American history. And then there's school *after* school. Of those who graduate college, nearly a third head to graduate school the following year.

In addition to choices surrounding higher education, your emerging adult faces a dizzying array of career choices. The average American now holds six *different jobs* between the ages of 18 to 26.[4] Which means that they may experience more job transition in the short span of a few years than previous generations did in their entire lifetime.

All of this job change—combined with looming student loans and a challenging economic climate—doesn't help the bank accounts of emerging adults (or yours, for that matter). As a result, your kid may take more time than you or your parents did to become financially independent.

Still, independence is their primary goal at this phase, which can explain why your kid makes the choices they do. Even when they play it cool, even when they act like they don't care that they're still living at home, emerging adults still feel anxiety and pressure to make it on their own—emotionally, intellectually, and relationally. They may not fully be adults yet, but they still want to be seen and taken seriously.

YOUR ROLE IN THIS PHASE IS TO MOBILIZE THEIR POTENTIAL

Even though their entire world revolves around *what's next,* many emerging adults have not thought about where they want to be in ten years. Some would like to have these conversations, and they need a safe place to share and process their thoughts—a place where they don't feel pressure to have it all figured out. Even if your kid isn't sure what they will do for a career or where the next step will take them, you can mobilize their potential by encouraging them to *invest in their identity capital*—the things they do to build who they are.

You can start by helping your son or daughter to pinpoint his or her passions, abilities, and interests.

Talk with them about where they would like to be when they are 30. Encourage them to invest in education, jobs, and experiences that can help them in that trajectory.

And if your kid doesn't always love having those conversations with you, that's okay. Sometimes they would rather talk with—and listen to—adults who aren't their parents. Suggest another adult who could be a good sounding board, like an uncle, a step-grandparent, a former youth pastor or small group leader, or a collegiate campus minister. No matter their age, your kid will always need to find older, wiser people who can help them navigate the next phase of life. Now is a great time to begin developing the skill of choosing those people and staying in contact with them.

THE UNIQUE CULTURAL CHOICES FACING YOUR DAUGHTER

Among those ages 18 to 33, women are six percent more likely to have finished at least a bachelor's degree than men. Today, 63 percent of young women are employed, while just 31 percent are not in the labor force.[5] Young adult women have more career choices than women had even a generation ago.

The challenge, however, is that women can feel the (often internal) pressure to "do it all." They may face the endless quest to balance career aspirations with family goals. This pressure can heighten feelings of insecurity, anxiety, and inadequacy. This is why emerging adult women are optimistic about maintaining balance, but also recognize and consider this tension between the professional and personal earlier and more intentionally than men.[6]

Be available to talk with your daughter about how these tensions affect her dreams. Celebrate the opportunities that come her way, and normalize the conflicting aspirations she feels. In a world where emerging adult women feel increasing and conflicting demands, you can be a safe place for her to process what's most important to her.

THE UNIQUE CULTURAL CHOICES FACING YOUR SON

Christian Smith, a sociologist who specializes in times of developmental transition, suggests that social pressures for men to be "tough" and "daring" still endure.

Today's emerging young men hear countless voices and opinions on what it means to be a man. They'll hear these voices from their peers, from culture, and from their parents. That's where you come in. Maleness in society is confusing and young people need older voices in their lives to encourage and inspire them to be responsible men.

When you talk with your son, ask questions that aren't just related to accomplishments, like grades or sports. Talk with them about their dreams, desires, pressures, and fears. Take time (more than once) to discuss risky behaviors and potentially negative outcomes. Ask them to walk through big social plans (like a party) or to role-play the situations they may find themselves in. Hold them accountable for their actions, and don't make excuses for any behavior that may harm them or others.

two

WHAT'S CHANGING RELATIONALLY

FRIENDS MATTER

Your kid's close relationships will change after high school. As they say goodbye to old friends and form new relationships in new places, keep in mind the following:

Goodbyes matter. Parents often focus on the upsides of graduating high school, talking with their kid about their new life and the new friends they'll make. Highlighting the positives of change is always helpful. But don't overlook the sense of loss your kid may feel as they say goodbye to their friends and familiar high school life. Acknowledge this loss with them. Encourage them to reflect on the great friends they've made. Talk with them about the fears they have of finding new friends. Remind them that their best friendships didn't happen overnight, but grew over the course of years. Encourage them that new relationships will take time to form as well.

New friendships matter. As your emerging adult transitions to college or their first job, they will meet people from different backgrounds than their family or friend groups. This will challenge and inspire them to develop new perspectives.[7] Remember that their evolving perspectives and opinions are partially informed by these new friendships. This means that when you have conversations, debates, or even arguments about religious, social, or political topics, your emerging adult is likely not just talking about the topic—they're connecting their ideas to someone they know and care about. Handle these topics with grace and tact.

LOVE AND SEX . . . AND EVENTUALLY MARRIAGE

In this phase, dating is increasingly complicated for your kid. You've probably heard the phrase "hooking up." This ambiguous term can mean everything from making out to intercourse. It can happen between "friends with benefits" or even relative strangers.

And while the idea of "hooking up" is based on casual, no-strings-attached sex, hookup culture isn't without its emotional side effects. Of those who engage in premarital sex, half of respondents report grief or regret over their early sexual activity.[8] So while it may feel awkward, it's still okay to encourage your emerging adult to make healthy life choices. We'll talk more about this later in the book. But for now, know that the awkward-conversation-stage isn't over just yet.

As your emerging adult moves through this phase, chances are they'll begin considering a long-term romantic relationship. Even though they may be thinking about this possibility, they're probably not in a hurry. In fact, the median age for *first marriage* is now 26.5 for women and 28.7 for men, both of which are more than five years later than the average fifty years ago.[9] And not only are emerging adults marrying later than previous generations, they're choosing to start families later as well.

In other words, the dating phase is lasting longer and becoming more complicated than ever before. This probably looks much different than the world you experienced. But that's okay. Now is a great time to get to know your kid's world by simply being curious. Ask questions without questioning choices. Show interest. Display genuine compassion for the relational challenges of this phase.

DIGITAL NATIVES AND DIGITAL IMMIGRANTS

The pace at which technology is changing has resulted in a generational gap between "Digital Immigrants" and "Digital Natives." If you remember a time before email, Google searches, social media, or phones smart enough to give you driving directions, you're officially a digital immigrant.

You may agree with computer scientist Alan Kay: "Technology is anything that was invented after you were born."[10]

On the other hand, your kid only knows the world as it exists in his or her lifetime—technology included. Smart devices, instant information, and constant connection are all part of the culture in which they grew up. They are digital natives.

As natives, they live and breathe technology. Tech skills come naturally to them. And the terms and language associated with technology don't feel as foreign to them as they may to you and me. A typical American emerging adult is engaged with media of some kind for about 12 hours daily. That's most of their waking hours.[11]

Parents often forget that their kid's media usage means something different to them than it does to you. Arguments that online social connections aren't "real life" relationships or somehow detract from real relationships fail to recognize the meaningful ways emerging adults use technology. Most texting and messaging done by your kid does not take away from relationships. Instead, this technology often fosters friendships.

Still, technology does pose some unique risks for digital natives. Your emerging adult sees countless images that reflect "perfection" or identify "failure."

One example? Social media often conveys unrealistic expectations about body image for both young women and men. These posts can unintentionally encourage eating disorders, chronic dieting, and unhealthy body expectations.

Excessive video gaming can also have negative social and psychological effects.

And constant access to pornography can lead to dangerous misperceptions of what a romantic relationship should look like.

So while the ground rules your kid had in high school for things such as screen time and Internet access may now seem condescending, there's nothing wrong with talking with them about how they use technology in light of their values and goals.

For example, if your child is in college and they don't seem to be performing to their best ability, ask them about how they use their free time. If he or she appears tired, ask about the daily routines they're keeping to ensure a healthy lifestyle.

And keep in mind, the temptation of social media is not only a "young person" dilemma. Do your best to be present when your children are present. When you go to dinner, or when you're doing something together, let your own behaviors set the tone. That may mean you put your phone away and model how to ignore the constant notifications from your device.

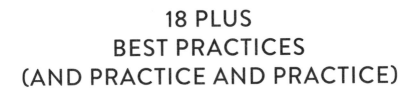

18 PLUS
BEST PRACTICES
(AND PRACTICE AND PRACTICE)

MANAGING AND LOCKBOXING

After spending one year studying high school seniors transitioning to their first year in college, sociologist Tim Clydesdale arrived at two major conclusions regarding young people who are leaving the adolescent phase and entering the emerging adult phase:[12]

"Daily life management" is the primary focus of young emerging adults. According to Clydesdale, young adults "manage the semi-adult relationships that now characterize their social interactions; they manage their adult freedoms to use substances and be sexually active, and they manage expanded responsibilities for their daily life, including money, food, and clothes." More than anything else, these daily concerns consume young adults during their first year out of high school.

Young emerging adults "lockbox" their identities until they are able to manage their daily lives.

During the first year or two after high school, emerging adults place their critical religious, political, racial, gender, and class identities in an internal "lockbox"—separate from their daily life—for safekeeping. The good news is that emerging adults value those identity roots enough to keep them protected. The bad news is that by not integrating their identities, they often fail to connect their choices, decisions, and lifestyles to who they are or what they value.

THE BIG FIVE OF EMERGING ADULTS

Having coined the term "emerging adult," psychologist Jeffrey Arnett argues that there are *five main features of emerging adulthood* that influence their outlook, emotions, and decisions:[13]

1. **Identity exploration:** They are trying out various life options with new freedom to move beyond previous traditions and habits.

2. **Instability:** They are revising and reshaping their patterns of love, work, and home.

3. **Self-focus:** They are emphasizing their own needs and obligations as they seek to be self-sufficient and stand on their own two feet.

4. **In-between:** They are feeling perpetually in transition, as neither adolescent nor adult.

5. **Possibilities:** They are sensing abundant hope with unparalleled opportunity to transform their lives.

WORKING 9 TO 5 . . . AND WHY

From a work/career perspective, Gallup's research confirms other findings on the importance of work and purpose at this phase:

- This generation wants to find purpose in their work. They want work to be meaningful and the organizations they work for to have purpose. This ideal motivates them more than money.

- They seek development and are looking for places to grow in their field.

- They desire continual feedback more than annual reviews, as they are used to continuous, almost immediate, reactions from others through social media.

- They believe their job and life are deeply connected, or want them to be.

NOT LEAVING CHURCHES AS MUCH AS SEEKING SUPPORTIVE ONES

In Christian circles, many parents are concerned that emerging adults are no longer attending church. Having studied over 250 congregations nationwide that are especially effective with 15-29-year-olds, the Fuller Youth Institute has identified *six core commitments of churches that are not growing old, but growing young.* Two of these commitments are especially relevant to your relationship with your emerging adult child:[14]

1. **The power of empathy.** The best congregations tear down any emotional or relational walls that commonly separate "us" (older generations) from "them" (young adults). By finding and highlighting what generations have in common, while also recognizing how the generations differ, these congregations earned the right to be heard after high school by first listening well.

2. **Warm is the new cool.** More than a cool worship space or a hip minister, young people want a place that feels like family. When it comes to emerging adults, warm is the new cool.

three

WHAT'S CHANGING PHYSICALLY

For many young adults, the puberty phase is (thankfully) over. While some young men may continue to grow physically for a few more years, the awkward stages of acne, hair growth, and weird smells are (mostly) behind them. But that doesn't mean your young adult is finished developing. Their bodies and brains are still changing. And while you mostly see the changes on the outside, a lot of new development is happening inside their brains.

You've heard the stories of the partying, the risky behaviors, and the bad influences. For parents, having a child enter college or get their first job can be both exciting and terrifying.

But *why*?

There are a lot of reasons. At this phase, your kid has . . .
more freedom than ever.
more temptations than before.
more desire to be their own person—and different from you—than they have ever experienced before.

And those new factors may push them to make decisions they wouldn't have made in earlier phases. But something else is changing, too. And it may play more of a role in their choices than we realize.

THE BRAIN'S RISKY BUSINESS

The human brain—which has been busy growing and developing since before birth—enters a new stage after high school. Adults think with a part of the brain called the prefrontal cortex. It's responsible for logic, reason, and making good decisions. Teenagers think with another part of their brain (the amygdala), and while that's changing in your emerging adult, the transition won't be fully complete until around age 25.[15]

Even though your kid is finding their way toward making better judgments, gaining more wisdom, and constructing their own worldview (thanks to the new developments in their prefrontal cortex), the part of their brain that allows them to take risks or try new things is a little ahead of the game. This is why . . .

- Embarking on an interstate road trip with friends at 2:00 a.m. feels like a great idea.
- Quitting a job—with no prospects of a new one—makes complete sense.
- Buying concert tickets, even though the checking account is empty, doesn't feel so crazy.
- Experimenting sexually at a weekend party seems completely natural.

On the outside, your kid looks less like a kid and more like an adult. But on the inside, their brain is still building the neurological pathways needed to make "adult" decisions.[16]

So add another reason to the "why your emerging adult child still needs you" list. Their brains aren't finished developing yet, which means they may have trouble making wise choices on their own. They need you—and otherwise, experienced adults—to help them process their thoughts and decisions.

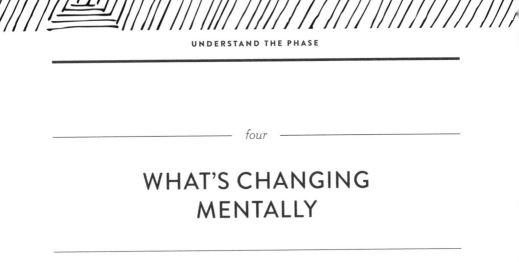

four

WHAT'S CHANGING MENTALLY

Whether your child is entering college or the workforce, they are novices in a world with far different requirements than high school—a world where learning and growth will be *their* responsibility.

LEARNING SEARCHES BEYOND "WHAT'S ON THE TEST"

Learning during the high school phase tends to be more passive. Teenagers go to school, do homework, and take tests because they have to. While they are learning along the way, they're often motivated by external factors such as grades (or, ahem, their parents).

In this post-graduate phase, however, emerging adults need encouragement to realize they're both capable of, *and* responsible for, their learning. Learning becomes more than writing what the instructor wants or knowing what will appear on the test. Instead, emerging adults are *learning to become learners*. And now, your grown-up kid needs to develop and maintain the ability and the desire to learn in order to keep up in a fast-changing world.

The goal? To help your kid keep learning and love learning.

Here are two ways to help them get there:

CHANGING THE WAYS YOU ASK QUESTIONS ABOUT THEIR LEARNING

If your young adult is in college, it will be tempting to ask them, "Did you get your homework done?" or "When is your next test?" Instead, try coming up with questions that value the learning process over the result. Ask questions like, "What's the most interesting thing you've been reading?" Or, "How is that political science class challenging some of your assumptions about the world?" Or, "What's one thing you've changed your mind about since starting college?" As they get older, many students find a newfound love of learning (sometimes bordering on obsession) with a particular topic or major. This is a great opportunity for you to value their ideas and model a love of learning by simply asking them to teach you about what they're discovering.

SHARE YOUR OWN LEARNING

Remember that high school student in your house who finally knew everything? Well, even adults are tempted to stop learning. (But you probably knew that already.) So keep stretching your own perspective. Read something challenging. Take a class or start lessons for something you've never tried. Then share your discoveries with your kid when the two of you are chatting. Show your young adult that learning never stops.

DID YOU KNOW?

One-fourth of young people claim that their generation's relationship with technology is what makes their generation unique.[19]

The generation born between 1980 and 2000 is more diverse than any other previous generation in US history. 44 percent report not being white.

Nine in 10 young adults report high levels of closeness with their parents and are happy with that relationship.[20]

Total student outstanding loan debt surpassed $1 trillion in 2014, making it the second largest category of household debt.[21]

Eighty percent of life's
most defining moments happen by age 35.[22]

Our personalities
change more in our 20s than any other time.[23]

Eighty percent of college students have an
interest in spirituality.[24]

Your emerging adult
has likely never licked a postage stamp.[25]

five

WHAT'S CHANGING EMOTIONALLY

Emotionally, the new opportunities available to emerging adults seem to make them a generally optimistic group. They see possibilities. Even in times of challenge, they're hopeful about their future relationships, jobs, and happiness.

TURNING THE PAGE

One of the best parts of this phase is a fresh start. Even if a kid loves high school, chances are there are some parts they wish they could change. Maybe they didn't have the best grades. Maybe they wish they had chosen better (or at least different) friends. Or maybe they're tired of being known for one thing or another. After graduation, the opportunity for a new start can offer a sense of optimism and endless possibilities.

At the same time, a new beginning can put young adults on shaky emotional ground, especially students who move away from their hometown. Living in a new place where no one knows them can cause insecurity. If they're not known as the smart kid, the athlete, the cheerleader, or the skater anymore, then who are they exactly? This question of identity, while healthy, can create a sense of anxiety.

So while your emerging adult is optimistic about the possibilities, he or she likely still needs some support from the few people who know them best.

six

WHAT'S CHANGING MORALLY

Following high school, your emerging adult is likely faced with new ideas and diverse perspectives that may challenge what they've always believed. At this phase, graduates are considering and reconsidering what is right and wrong, and what that means for them personally.

FROM THE OUTSIDE IN

When your kid was little, their motivation was simple. If they did the right thing, you rewarded them. If they did the wrong thing, you punished them. Generally, a single voice shaped their morality: you.

But as they got older, a growing number of voices began to influence your child's moral decisions. From people like . . .

Teachers
Administrators
Coaches
Sunday School teachers
The boss at their part-time job

Basically, any authority figure could motivate kids to make good, moral decisions. That begins to change during this phase, as **moral decisions move from external to internal.**

You may see your emerging adult begin to make more decisions out of internal motivations like personal values, beliefs, and convictions. Ultimately, that's a good thing, as morality becomes less about "What can

I get away with?" and more about "What do I believe and what kind of person do I want to be?"

At the same time, your kid may begin to develop beliefs, values, and moral positions that may or may not agree with your own. And if your son or daughter rejects some of your views, it's easy to feel like they're rejecting *you*. But they're not.

They now want to take ownership for what and why they believe. And ultimately, you *want* your kid's thought process to move from simply "what adults tell me" to "what I think for myself." The win-win for you and your emerging adult is not to fight over each other's moral positions, but to encourage them (and you!) to explain your process of arriving at your conclusions. And then *listen*. Listen to your young adult's perspective. **Because when it comes to leading young adults, *dialogue* is better than debate.**

THREE QUESTIONS THAT CAN SHAPE YOUR KID'S VIEW OF MORALITY AND THEIR DECISIONS

Emerging adults often find new motivations as they wrestle with three major moral questions, and attempt to pin down *their own* answers regarding identity, belonging, and purpose.

Who am I?
The question of identity, or "Who am I?" is part of every life stage. But this question grows louder as kids enter adulthood. For your emerging adult, this question may also bring up other big questions about who God is and how they were made. When your young adult understands that they're created in God's image and saved by His grace, this knowledge can give them a sense of place and value in the world.

Where do I belong?
Your emerging adult child is beginning to ask deeper questions about belonging. In other words, "Where is my place and who are my people?" This question often leads them to consider, maybe unconsciously, the purpose of church, whether they need church, and what it means to participate in a faith community. As they move away from your spiritual habits and live out their own moral convictions, they'll eventually decide whether or not to be part of a church or a faith community.

Why am I here?

Emerging adults begin to ask profound questions about what they love to do and the contribution they want to make in their world. Ultimately, they'll need to discover the answer for themselves. But your kid will benefit from the support of caring adults who can guide them and help them refine their life's purpose and calling. Recognize that you can play an exciting role in helping your kid find identity beyond image, belonging beyond a peer group, and purpose beyond a profession. Ask them about these questions and weave the threads of identity, belonging, and purpose into your regular conversations.

LEVERAGE THE PHASE

SIX THINGS YOUR EMERGING ADULT NEEDS

LEVERAGE IT

Now that you know more about your emerging adult, you might be wondering, "What does all this mean for how I parent?" Your role with your young adult continues to change Week 937 and beyond.

We believe every child needs you to leverage six things over time:

LOVE, WORDS, STORIES, WORK, FUN, and TRIBES.

You don't have to accomplish all six at once.

And there are no formulas or guarantees (you've been parenting long enough to know that!).

But these six areas offer you some great initial steps to start journeying with your emerging adult into this next phase.

TIME MATTERS

We don't have to convince you that time matters.

We definitely don't have to convince you that time goes fast.

If you've been following along with any of the other Phase books, you know that we encourage parents to keep a jar of marbles—936 marbles to be exact. That's the exact number of weeks a parent has between their child's birth and high school graduation. Removing a marble each week is a great way to mark the time and remind ourselves of this simple truth:

When we realize how much time we have left, we do more with the time we have now.

At this phase, your marble jar is empty. There are no more weeks to count down. But that doesn't mean your time is up! Obviously, age 18 doesn't mark the end of your relationship with your kid. Instead, it's the beginning of your *new* relationship with your adult child.

We have discovered that right around the time the marbles run out, parents are tempted to respond in one of two ways:

Some check out—believing that their parenting is done. They assume they have no more influence in their kids' lives, so they keep their distance, not wanting to meddle in their kids' business.

Some hold on—unable to really let go, either out of fear for their child or out of fear for themselves! These well-meaning parents hover right into the emerging adult years, managing schedules, finances, and relationships, doing whatever it takes to keep their kid . . . well . . . a kid. But when parents continue to relate to their young adult as if they are a child, they're missing out on getting to know their new adult.

Here's a spoiler: neither approach is helpful.

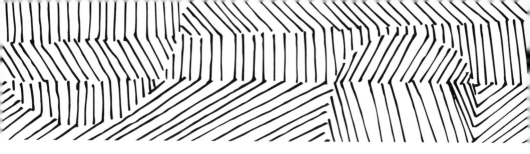

Just like with any new relationship, you will need to spend time with your emerging adult, as the two of you learn to relate to one another in a whole different way. When you choose to spend time with someone, you create a shared experience. And when you do that over time, you create a history—not just a history with the little kid you raised, but a personal history with the newly emerging adult they are now.

In other words, time / time = history.

So find some ways to spend time with your new emerging adult.

Look for opportunities to connect casually through texts of affirmation.

Meet for lunch, just to enjoy each other's company. Dispel their fear that "lunch" means "interrogation" (and prove it by your actions).

Take a trip as a family, or just the two of you.

Establish new traditions that honor their new life rhythms.

Keep being intentional about making memories.

And be flexible and gracious.

Your experience together during this "emerging" phase will be the foundation on which you build your new adult relationship.

6 THINGS KIDS (AND EMERGING ADULTS) NEED OVER TIME

LOVE/TIME = WORTH

WORDS/TIME = DIRECTION

STORIES/TIME = PERSPECTIVE

WORK/TIME = SIGNIFICANCE

FUN/TIME = CONNECTION

TRIBES/TIME = BELONGING

one

LOVE/TIME = WORTH

"As young people, we are surrounded by expectations that may have little to do with who we really are, expectations held by people who are not trying to discern our selfhood but to fit us into slots."

— **Parker J. Palmer**
Let Your Life Speak: Listening for the Voice of Vocation

For over 18 years, you've told your child that you love them. If anyone told you anything for 18 years straight, you'd remember it. And you'd probably believe them. So is it even possible, at this point, that our kids don't know or feel that we love them?

Well, maybe.

See, someone else has been talking to them for 18 years, too. As long as they can remember, they have been receiving messages from culture, school, work, art, drama, and sports that reinforce another idea: Love and worth are connected to performance. And while they're probably convinced that you have to love them because you're their parent, it can be tempting for them to wonder if you love who they are now—especially if who they are now doesn't line up with who they know you imagined them to be.

If you want kids and teenagers to . . . have a healthy sense of self-worth, believe in a Creator who loves them unconditionally, discover the value of using their lives to love others, then you may have to get in the business of actually proving that you love them—no matter what.

— *Losing Your Marbles / Playing For Keeps*

AFFIRM WHERE THEY ARE

One of the best ways to prove you love an emerging adult is to affirm who they are and where they are right now. Of course, it's easier to affirm *where* they are if they're currently where we *want* them to be.

With the best of motives, you might find yourself thinking (and saying), "I didn't raise you that way," or "Don't go liberal on me," or "I didn't invest all of that money for you to do *that*," or "You didn't act like this when you were little." You might think you're being helpful. But in their eyes, you seem disappointed in what they do. And maybe worse, disappointed in *who they are*.

Out of fear—and with good intentions—parents may try to control, manipulate, or coerce their kids. And as they attempt to live their own lives, emerging adults experiment, disregard, or rebel.

It's at this point you have a choice.

You can fight with your kid . . . a lot.
Or you can fight for your relationship with them.

Love/time means letting go of your dreams for who your child could
become or marry. It means relinquishing your hopes for where they might
be by the time they are 19. . . or 25.

Emerging adults don't need critiques, they need *interest*. Before their
choices are labeled as different, odd, or wrong, your emerging adult
needs you to be courageous enough to try and understand the world from
their perspective. They need you to ask questions, not make judgments.
They need you to wonder *with* them, not place more pressure *on* them.

LET LOVE OVERRIDE YOUR FEARS

Of course you love your kid. But if you're like most parents, you probably
get anxious sometimes.

Maybe during their high school years you wondered if they would get
the right GPA, or get the scholarship, or have the right activities for their
college applications. Maybe you wondered if they would get into the
"right" college (or *any* college).

When it comes to guiding your child toward higher education, the
situation can be stressful.

But that concern doesn't stop at high school graduation. Once your son
or daughter leaves for college, you might begin to worry about their life
post-college or when they will . . .

start dating someone.
stop dating everyone.
get a job.
get a better job.
move out.
pay for themselves.
take care of themselves.

The problem is, **when you parent out of fear,
it can mask your good intentions.**

You begin to ask questions like, "What will you do about . . ?" and "What happens if . . ?" Well-intentioned comments like these may add to the pressure your kid is already facing. Questions that are meant to be empowering may sound judgmental. Suggestions may feel suffocating. And you may hear them saying, "Stop worrying," or "I've got this," even when you're sure they don't.

Love, in this phase, means you may need to . . .

listen more than you advise.
journey with them more than plan for them.
choose trust over suspicion.
believe the best about them (and say good things about them) even when they mess up.

In this phase, love takes the role of a cheerleader, not an evaluator.

AVOID BEING A DRONE

After being present in high school (maybe a little too present), "helicopter parents" have graduated to college with their children. But now they've become "drone parents." A drone parent may not be physically present, but they can still follow and track their child through email, texts, and social media. And if the child needs them to help or intervene, the parent is poised to jump in and attack the problem. Immediately. And with precision.

"The problem," as one parent shared, "is that our kids who are in their 20s are living their lives through social media, where they succeed and fail out loud." And even if your young adult is fine airing their failures in public, you might want them kept private. You want to spare your child the pain of stumbling in public. And you'd like to spare *yourself* the pain of watching them fall.

So you remind them that their English Literature paper is due next week.

And then you remind them again three days later.

And when they fail the paper, you contact the professor to argue for a better grade.

In other words, **drone parents become personal assistants for emerging adults who aren't being given much chance to "emerge" or "adult" at all.**

Or maybe you've gone to the other parenting extreme. Maybe you're so determined to avoid drone parenting that you minimize contact. No texts. No emails. No direct messages. It's time for your child to sink or swim. And it's not your job to provide a life preserver.

But something doesn't feel quite right about that either. You still care. Deeply. Your gut tells you that healthy parenting doesn't mean radio silence.

So as you try to find the loving middle ground between droning and disengaging, think about the following questions. And maybe even talk about them with your son or daughter.

- Whether your adult child leaves home or has a schedule where you rarely see them, what are your expectations for keeping in touch?

- Is it okay to follow your son or daughter and their friends on social media?

- How will you talk with them about their school, work, and relationships?

- If your son or daughter asks for help, how will you approach the situation that helps them problem-solve, not just solve their problem?

- What do your interactions with your adult child communicate about what you think of them? What might be positive? What might be painful?

two

WORDS/TIME = DIRECTION

"Forget the logistics and take the opportunity to bless them. They want your blessing, not your to-do list."

— **College President**

Words are a big deal. They have the power to tell us who we are and shape our life direction. Think about this in your own life. Good or bad, what words have shaped you?

"If you want a kid to know they matter, then it matters what words you use when you talk to them and about them. The words you use can set them up to feel . . . Significant, Valued, Unique"

— Reggie Joiner / Kristen Ivy
Playing for Keeps

As your emerging adult walks into a season of the unknown, more than ever, he or she needs someone to tell them not what to do—but who they are.

WEIGH WHAT YOU SAY

When parents feel out of control, they default to asking their kids about logistics. A parent who's nervous about an upcoming camping trip may ask questions about details ("Did you pack sunscreen?") or their itinerary ("Are you leaving early enough to avoid traffic?").

This is also true during major 18+ transitions. One college president noticed year after year that parents dropping off their freshmen were preoccupied with logistical questions. Nervous parents use to-do lists to calm their anxiety.

At one of our (Steve's) daughter's freshman send-offs, the college president invited parents to make the most of the moment by affirming their children, telling them that they believe in them and that they love them. I'll admit it— there were hugs, more tears than I anticipated, and awkwardness, but we could feel the love in the room. And I realized that this is what my daughter would hold onto in college, not her to-do list.

Ultimately, how you talk with your kid lets them know how you feel about them *and* what you believe about them. Words of affirmation will let them know you believe they can handle adulthood. Words focused on logistics can communicate the opposite.

That doesn't mean we should never give them logistical advice! After all, at some point they'll need to know they can't do three weeks of laundry in one load. But we can decide to *not* let those be the words that show up most often. We can weigh our words to make sure the ones that get repeated are the ones we want running through their minds.

This advice isn't just for parents of freshmen. Young adults at all stages of the journey need their parents' words. They need heartfelt words of love, support, and encouragement, not logistical advice.

LEARN A NEW LANGUAGE

Use age-matching vocabulary.
Even though you know your kid is older, you might still default to speaking to them as if they were 16. For example, you may be accustomed to saying to your high school child, "Where are you going and will you be home by midnight?" For young adults, try to rephrase the question to honor their autonomy and still show your interest: "Hey, just to keep all of our schedules straight, would you tell me your plans and when you think you'll be home?" Remind them that this is the way adults talk with each other to navigate life together. It's not about being nosy.

In addition to choosing age-appropriate ways of talking to your emerging adult, here are a couple sentence-starters to avoid:

"When I was your age . . . "
Everybody loves a sentence that starts this way.

Okay, no. No one likes hearing this phrase. At best, it sounds critical. At worst, it sounds condescending. Either way, when you say this to your young adult, they're automatically going to be defensive.

The irony is that we usually say this in an attempt to relate to adult children. Our memories of our 20s are more recent than our teenage years and likely more familiar to a young adult. Still, our twenty-something experiences have little in common with the world of today's emerging adults. Your attempt to compare or equate your kid's current life with your own experience will likely alienate rather than connect.

So instead of talking about how you did things back in the day (the right and better way, of course), look for opportunities to ask your kid about their own experiences through phrases like:

- "What it's like to be in college right now?"
- "What are you most excited or scared about as you graduate and look for a job?"
- "What do you appreciate about your friends, and who do you think you'll stay closest with?"
- "How do you think your life may be different than when I was your age? How might it be the same?"

"When are you going to . . ?"
Parents in this phase are often obsessed with results, constantly asking when their young adult is going to . . .

Move out
Get a job
Get married

A more helpful approach? Talk with them about their plans to achieve the goals *they* desire. More meaningful conversations may start with questions like:

- "When do you imagine living on your own, and what can we do to support your goal?"
- "Getting a job can be hard. What can we do to help you prepare for interviews?"
- "I'm/We're going out for dinner tonight. Would you and your friend like to join us?"

three

STORIES/TIME = PERSPECTIVE

SHARE STORIES THAT INSPIRE THEM

"*I think life is staggering and we're just too used to it.*"

— **Donald Miller**
A Million Miles in a Thousand Years: What I Learned While Editing My Life

TELL FAMILY STORIES

During the holiday season, a group named Story Corps encourages adolescents and emerging adults to interview their older relatives about their lives and family history to "record and share the stories that are all around you." Since 2003, they have captured over 60,000 interviews.

Why? Because stories matter.

At a church that regularly partners with the Fuller Youth Institute, church leaders remind themselves that, "In order to know where we are going, we need to know where we've been."

And that may be just as true for a young adult.

It can be tempting to believe that your kid is still just as resistant to hearing "old stories" as they were when they were younger, but that isn't necessarily true. The more they begin to understand their own present and future, the more they want (and need) to know about their past. As a parent, you're a curator of those stories. Some ways to naturally and organically share about the past (both yours and theirs) are to start conversations like this:

- "Do you know how we got to live in this part of the country?"
- "Can I tell you why I went into [banking, construction, teaching, etc.]?"
- "Do you know how your mom/dad and I met?"
- "Have you ever heard Grandma's/Grandpa's story?"
- "One of the best times in my life was . . ."
- "One of the hardest times in my life was . . ."
- "Do you know why we carry on that tradition?"

Don't ever assume that your kid already knows the family stories. Tell as much as you can or think is appropriate. Emphasize the bumps along the way, not just the (somewhat) perfect finish.

SHARE FAITH STORIES

Researcher Christian Smith notes that for many Christian families, the language of faith has become a lost language. It's not that parents and their kids don't *want* to talk about spiritual things. Rather, they've *lost the ability* to talk about them.

The good news is that it is never too late to have a faith conversation (or a lot of them) with your young adult. This kind of conversation just needs someone to go first.

And that someone is you.

While it's sometimes unusual or awkward for families to talk about faith, an easy way to share your own faith story is to say to them, "You know, I don't think I've ever told you how I got to the point where faith was important to me. Do you want to hear my story?" Be as open as you want and let them ask questions about your journey.

Expect them to believe differently.
Parents often assume that if their kids are not expressing their faith in the exact same way as them, their children are leaving faith entirely. More likely, emerging adults are learning how to express their faith through their own personalities, language, and life experiences.

Rather than allowing this to become a point of contention, talk openly about your similarities and differences. Two great questions to ask include:

- "What do you not believe anymore that you think I still believe?"
- "What do you believe that you think I don't believe?"

Give them permission to name what might be different. Let that be a place for honest and deep conversation that leads to better understanding between you.

PROVIDE THEM WITH FAMILY MEDICAL HISTORY

Up to this point, you likely have been the ones to keep track of your children's medical history, and they may still be on your insurance. Emerging adults need to know their own medical history so that they can advocate for themselves when they see doctors. Doctors ask about family medical history and your children should know essential information. Spend time with them and get them up to date on the following:

- The basics of their health history, such as their last physical, as well as their history of immunizations, eye exams, and dental treatments
- Any family history of disease, such as diabetes, cancer, alcoholism, or depression
- Their insurance plans and/or options
- How to make medical and dental appointments
- How to pick up prescriptions from the pharmacy
- How to pay medical bills
- Who has power of attorney if medical decisions need to be made
- Who they can call if they have medical questions

four

WORK/TIME = SIGNIFICANCE

HELP THEM CLARIFY THEIR LAUNCH INTO A CAREER

"The lottery question might get you thinking about what you would do if talent and money didn't matter. But they do. The question twenty somethings need to ask themselves is what they would do with their lives if they didn't win the lottery."

— **Meg Jay**
The Defining Decade: Why Your Twenties Matter - And How to Make the Most of Them Now

Watching your kid join the working world is one of the most exciting parts of parenting a young adult—mostly because they're now off your payroll. As a parent, it's like getting an automatic raise! But even if your child isn't certain about a long-term career yet, work is still important.

Whether work looks like . . .
a part-time job.
an unpaid internship.
volunteering in the community.
serving at church.
getting an entry level job in a new field.

It's all important because any kind of work can help a kid see their impact on the world around them.

And while work for your emerging adult now looks different than taking out the garbage or helping with the family pet, it still has the same effect: Work, over time, helps a young adult discover their purpose.

CONSIDER A GAP YEAR

Sometimes emerging adults don't neatly fit the traditional trajectory of "high school then college then job." This realization, coupled with a wider range of opportunities, gives emerging adults more choices on their path toward adulthood.

One popular option is taking a gap year before or after college. Positively, gap-year travel has been shown to enhance confidence, knowledge, and skills relevant for future employment. It gives young people opportunities to take more time to reflect on their beliefs and attitudes as they work to make sense of who they are and where they want to invest themselves. Even prestigious institutions like Princeton University offer what they call "The Bridge Year Program," allowing admitted students to defer a year to serve the community with university support.

Used strategically, a gap year may be exactly what your young adult needs. Used haphazardly, a gap "year" can turn into a string of experiences or "years" that distract them from their journey toward identity, belonging, and purpose. So if a gap year makes sense for your young adult, talk with them about when this year starts, ends, and what they plan to do next. All gap years need to fit into an overall life plan.

TALK ABOUT POSSIBLE CAREERS

At some point in adulthood, your son or daughter will transition from "student" to "career person." Undergraduates transitioning to work often go through a three-stage process:

- *Anticipation* is the period before they join an organization, as they imagine what work will be and what they will leave behind as a student.

- *Adjustment* is the time of entry as a new employee when they feel the pressure to establish themselves as a valuable worker and develop new skills and relationships.

- *Achievement* is when they have evaluated their place in the organization and feel a growing sense of commitment and satisfaction.

As you can imagine, this process often gets disrupted. Poor preparation hurts anticipation, hard transitions can hurt adjustment, and failure can deny achievement. At every step of the way, you can serve as a supportive sounding board that helps them carefully think about their aspirations, experiences, and interpretations. Given that fewer than half of college-educated employees have the same job two years after graduation, your child's first job is as much about investing in their identity as it is about their success.

REGROUP BEFORE RELAUNCHING

One unexpected experience for parents is when their kid comes home after being away at school, at work, at military boot camp, or away on a trip. Whether your emerging adult is visiting temporarily or is part of the 40 percent of this generation that moves back home to live with you, they have changed.

So have you.

They have developed new patterns.

So have you.

Complicating this dynamic, different ethnic cultures often have particular expectations regarding child/parent relationships and living arrangements that must also be navigated.

Whatever the arrangement, your goal is that everyone is clear about the ground rules. Here are some questions that parents and emerging adults should discuss before kids move back in:

1. *Does your son or daughter have a plan while living at home—more education, networking, or job searching? Are those ventures full-time, part-time, or volunteer?*

2. *Is there a goal or end date (e.g., a month, no more than a year), or is it open-ended?*

3. *Will they pay rent, contribute to household expenses, or provide regular help with errands, grocery shopping, and cleaning?*

4. *Will they prepare or help with meals?*

5. *Will they do their own laundry?*

6. *Will they be allowed to use your car?*

7. *Do they need to call/text when they'll be gone for dinner or out past a certain time?*

8. *Can romantic partners come over? Sleep over?*

9. *Can they smoke or use alcohol around the house?*

The purpose of these questions is not to offend emerging adults and their independence. The purpose is to clarify expectations for living in community—specifically, the community of your home—know that along the way, expectations will need to be discussed, renegotiated, and adjusted.

five

FUN/TIME = CONNECTION
PLAY AND LAUGH TOGETHER

"The man who goes alone can start today; but he who travels with another must wait till that other is ready."

— **Henry David Thoreau**

PURSUE THEM IN NEW WAYS

I (Steve) remember talking with a younger father who was commenting on how exhausted he was because his young child kept coming into his study asking him to play. This young dad had expressed his fatigue to an older dad who responded, "Remember that one day, they'll stop coming to your room to ask you to play." Wanting to remember this reality, the younger father taped a quote on his door: "They won't knock forever."

It's true. Somewhere along the way, children stop pursuing parents. Wise parents of emerging adults recognize that it's *their turn* to pursue their children.

Your son or daughter wants a good relationship with you. They might not have the energy or drive to be proactive, so you need to be creative in pursuing your child.

If your emerging adult lives in town, or when she or he comes to town, seek them out and make the most of the interaction time you get with them. Treat each encounter as a chance to keep growing in your relationship.

ASK FOR HELP

Is there something that you want to grow in, develop, or accomplish? It's possible your emerging adult is actually good (or at least better than you) at that task. Allow them to be the expert and invite them into your process. Ask them to help you:

- Get connected with social media
- Develop a website
- Run a 5K
- Go on a biking tour
- Learn about an artist
- Read fiction or non-fiction
- Take a class
- Follow a podcast

GET OUT OF TOWN

The end of high school doesn't have to mean the end of family trips. One of the best ways to draw parents and all the siblings together is to head out of town. Now that your kid is out of high school and out of the house, this type of trip will require some extra planning and schedule coordination.

Getting away to a different destination—the woods, a lake, another country—helps everyone disconnect from daily routines and social media and re-connect with each other. On a trip, "family time" doesn't just happen when it's planned. It's a permanent state.

And this trip doesn't have to be extravagant. Camping, swapping homes with another family, staying in a nearby hotel, or even "staycations" at home can all accomplish the same goal: family time that matters. Let your emerging adult know your family budget (and maybe even have them contribute as they become able) and see what creative ideas they may have.

ACT NOW

Now that your child is out of high school, you might find yourself attending fewer of their events. Likely there are less games and recitals and plays. Maybe you look around and think, *I have free time!*

You might even have *more* schedule flexibility than your kid.

This newfound availability gives you the chance to be both relational and spontaneous. Too many conversations between parents and emerging adults end with, "We should get together sometime." Try not to let your conversations end this way. Instead, suggest something tangible and, if possible, immediate:

- "Want to grab dinner tonight?"
- "I've got an extra ticket to the game on Saturday. Want to go?"
- "I can grab coffee now."
- "I'm in the neighborhood. Need anything?"

Don't worry if it doesn't work out, and be careful not to communicate pressure or obligation. Continue to let them know that you're thinking of them and enjoy being with them. Enjoy the moments when the stars (and your schedules) align and you get that special time together.

VARY YOUR CONVERSATION TOPICS

When you get together with your adult son or daughter, it's tempting to pummel them with questions about their schoolwork, job, finances, relationships, and responsibilities. Without your intending it, your child suddenly feels like they're being interrogated. This scenario is exciting on TV. In real life? Not so much. Who wants to feel like every conversation is a confrontation?

Those questions are needed and important,
but also try to vary your topics.

- Talk about your interests or people you care about.
- Discuss current events, politics, or other subjects that interest you both.
- Laugh.
- Talk about dreams (without defaulting to jobs).
- Enjoy the silence.

six

TRIBES/TIME = BELONGING
HELP THEM EXPERIENCE COMMUNITY

"We have all known the long loneliness and we have learned that the only solution is love and that love comes with community."

— **Dorothy Day**
The Long Loneliness:
The Autobiography of the
Legendary Catholic Social Activist

FIND NEW COMMUNITY

Your emerging adult is embarking on a new, and maybe foreign, adventure. They're leaving the familiar relationships and patterns of home and pursuing their studies, work, or military service in new locations. They're building and finding new community.

For some young adults, this is an exciting time to branch out, or even start over. For others, this is a process of letting go and grieving the connections they've taken for granted. In this new phase, your son or daughter will encounter new people with different backgrounds, new groups that value a variety of causes, and new social clusters that may build them up or tear them down. Chances are that their early emerging adult years will produce some of the deepest friendships your kid will have—relationships that often last a lifetime.

For you, this may be the first time that you learn about their new friends and relationships from a distance. Chances are you will not know their friends' histories, parents, or stories. You will need to be attentive in order to see your emerging adult's friend groups through their eyes. You will learn to discover what your kid values about their new community. And, chances are, you'll learn even more about your emerging adult who is making their own relational choices.

But this new dynamic doesn't mean you no longer have influence. In this phase, your influence can expand beyond your own kid. As you connect with their friends, you can even influence their entire tribe. Now, instead of just being the adult who asks them to please shut the door so bugs don't get in the house, you may be seen as a supportive adult "parent." You may become a wise outside voice to other young adults who need a place to belong.

CREATE SAFE INTERGENERATIONAL SPACES

Young adults tend to spend most of their time with people their own age. While this can be an important season of peer-ness, many are eager for interactions with those different—and older—than them. They long for help in asking the questions they do not yet know how to ask.

Using your home, you can create an environment that allows for intergenerational encounters and safe conversation. As much as you are willing, make your home a welcome space for your kid's friends. Treat them like, and engage them, as adults. They're not adolescents anymore, which allows you to foster new and deeper conversations if they're willing.

Many parents have found that younger adults love to gather for brunch or dinner. Time and conversation over a meal offers support and connection that they might not find anywhere else.

ENCOURAGE YOUR CHURCH TO DEFINE THEIR RELATIONSHIP WITH EMERGING ADULTS

It's a common belief that emerging adults have left the church. We wonder, however, if it's possible that the church has left *them*.

Young adults seek answers to deep questions about the complex world around them.

They have visions of changing this world.

Sadly, emerging adults often fall into a gap between "youth ministry" and "adult ministry." But these young adults are more than their marital status and need more from their church than a place to meet other singles.

They want to know what their relationship with the church looks like. And what it means. And if they belong there.

They want to know if their voice matters and if they can trust their faith community with their questions, concerns, and challenges.

Emerging adults need leaders and adults in the church community to create space for them to participate, serve, grow, create, and express their faith.

We believe that the church should be one of the best places for a young adult to find belonging. Unfortunately, in this phase, finding a church, and finding one where they *feel* like they belong, can be a challenge.

So instead of reminding them, "You should be in church" or asking, "Did you go to church this Sunday?" try asking questions like . . .

- "What kind of church would you like to attend?"
- "Who could go with you if you visited a new church?"
- "Is there an area of the church where you think you'd like to volunteer?"
- "Are any of the churches in your area known for having a great college or young adult ministry?"
- "What are the on-campus faith organizations like at your school? Do any of them interest you?"

NOT LIKE IT USED TO BE

One of the key words for describing friendship in this phase is *changing*. Many emerging adults who have come out of familiar friendships nurtured in high school and college find it challenging to connect with and develop new friend groups. For high school graduates, seeking friendships is a crucial priority. For college graduates, creating friendships outside the natural rhythms of campus life requires a whole new way of thinking. Some worry that "it's not like it used to be." Sharing life together with people who have similar lifestyles has vanished. Their lives are now dictated by responsibilities that pull them away from—not toward—each other.

This new relational reality can make friendship and dating more complex and complicated. A parent can help by acknowledging this change, the loss they feel, and the hopes they have. Here are some dos and don'ts:

- **DO** empathize. Give them space to reflect and to grieve over what they miss about their high school and college friendships.
- **DON'T** suggest people they should be friends with.
- **DO** encourage them by brainstorming ways for them to develop new friend groups by finding common interest connections through environments like church, theater, or athletic groups.
- **DON'T** ask them when they're going to date or get married.

CELEBRATE THE PHASE

—

THE BIG MOMENTS

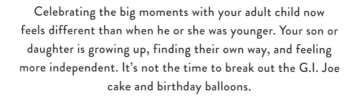

Celebrating the big moments with your adult child now feels different than when he or she was younger. Your son or daughter is growing up, finding their own way, and feeling more independent. It's not the time to break out the G.I. Joe cake and birthday balloons.

Still, these are opportunities to mark important moments and to reaffirm your love and support for your child. The goal is not to make milestone events as big as possible, but as meaningful as possible. Think of these moments as opportunities to say to your emerging adult . . .

I SEE SO MANY GREAT THINGS IN YOU.

YOU SHOW ME THINGS ABOUT THE WORLD I'VE NEVER SEEN BEFORE.

I ENJOY YOU AS A PERSON.

I'M INSPIRED BY YOU.

I'M EXCITED FOR YOU.

I LOVE WHO YOU ARE BECOMING.

I'M FOR YOU.

one

BIRTHDAYS

18 LOOKING BOTH BACKWARD AND FORWARD

At 18, your son or daughter may still live at home, but is probably thinking about life beyond home.

Their 18th birthday may be one of the last with your kid fully at home. The amount of "up close" time you have with your child from this birthday forward will shrink each year.

So take advantage of this pivotal birthday.

Don't smother.

But take some time to reflect on your life together. Use this birthday to look both *backward and forward.*

Host a small party with your immediate family. Share publicly with the group the qualities you appreciate in your child, as well as what you love about them. Speak empowering words to them. Write them a card. Make a video.

There are almost certainly adults who have significantly shaped your child over their first 18 years. Invite these lifelong family friends, relatives, teachers, coaches, pastors, neighbors, or mentors to send notes that affirm your emerging adult.

If your kid has a party with friends, encourage them to somehow mark the moment. Take a picture and have it framed. Cover a wall with paper and have everyone write down memories, wishes, or funny stories. Sign a basketball, a musical score, or a t-shirt.

Your kid's 18th birthday is a crucial moment when home life is ending—or at least changing—and new chapters are opening. Do your part by speaking words that matter with the people who have mattered to them the most.

21 CHEERING FOR ALL THE RIGHT REASONS

With all of the cultural clichés around turning 21, it's no wonder that this birthday can elevate parents to a new level of anxiety. "Celebrating" 21 can often lead to poor choices and painful outcomes. And because of your kid's new reality, if they're not living at home, it's tempting to think there's nothing you can do to prevent a celebration from going wrong.

Which means it's also tempting to avoid talking with your almost-21-year-old about what they're planning for that big day.

But remember, when you fail to have a conversation, your son or daughter is left with a void. They are left with only what TV, movies, and music paint as the perfect 21st birthday celebration. Or they only hear the uninformed "guidance" of other 21-year-olds whose brains are still learning to regulate adventurous thinking.

This can also be a great moment to remind them that you are there for them *no matter what*, and that they can reach out for help or support *no matter what*.

On a more positive note, the privileges of turning 21 can offer you a window to catch up and bond with your child. If drinking alcohol with your son or daughter is not appropriate or contrasts with your religious tradition, that's okay. You don't have to hit up a local bar together. But because 21 is such a celebrated (even idolized) birthday in American culture, try to develop an alternative milestone that appeals to your kid. Invest time in thinking about a special event that can be meaningful to both you and your child. Book a night in a downtown hotel and explore the city together. Take them to a concert or musical or game. Spend a day visiting their favorite coffee houses, restaurants, and hang-out spots. Invite their friends and get to know them, too!

Twenty-one is not just any birthday. It's a milestone. So make it feel that way. Celebrate your new 21-year-old and have some fun together.

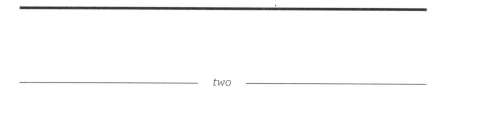

two

HOLIDAYS

Your emerging adult no longer lives at home, but you still want to pull the family together for the holidays. If it's been a while since you've seen your kid, you're tempted to pull even tighter than normal. Your control dial may move from a 4 to a 9.

That? Not so wonderful.

As your young adult is learning to manage new expectations, time commitments, and opportunities, holiday schedules can be tricky to navigate. That means holidays are a great time for you to demonstrate some new, enlightened flexibility.

Maybe you're thinking, "Flexibility is great. I can be so flexible. Unless they're missing the tree lighting. Or the cookie decorating. Or the annual viewing of *Home Alone*. That's *not* going to happen." We get it. With so much changing in your family, holiday traditions can begin to feel sacred and necessary.

On the other hand, if you think about it, your traditions only exist because somewhere, sometime, someone in your family chose to do something different from their previous tradition. Traditions are the product of breaking tradition. So while you don't want to throw all nostalgia out the window, this season of life is a great time to embrace new traditions as a family and maybe even let go of some old ones.

Making a list, checking it twice.

What are your assumptions about holidays? Do you assume that your child will come home? That's understandable. But it may not be a reality for Christmas, Thanksgiving, The Fourth of July, Presidents Day, *and* Groundhog Day. Your emerging adult may, in fact, want to come home for these holidays, but work, school, or military responsibilities might make that impossible.

You may need to adjust the timing of your traditions. A turkey on the day after Thanksgiving can taste just as good as it does on the official day. And without the pressure of the holiday, the conversations might even be better.

If your kid wants to bring a friend or significant other to a holiday gathering, let them. Anyone who is that special to your child is someone you want to get to know.

Forcing your plan or shaming them into doing "what we always do" may get you one or two holiday traditions that are important to you, but it may cost you far more in terms of participation, engagement, and relational time. If you win the battle but lose the war, you really haven't won much at all.

Decorations matter. And they don't.

I (Steve) remember coming home from college at winter break and walking into a home filled with decorations and smells of the season. My mom's holiday work signaled to me that I was "home."

But there was a greater sign of home than the decorations, the events, or the busyness. (I had just finished finals at school and was all done with "busy.") I knew I was home when my mom took time to hang out with me when I had "nothing to do." Or when she stayed up later than normal to greet me when I returned home after a late night out with friends.

I was happy those decorations greeted me. But I was happier that, since my mom had done that work ahead of time, she could truly *be with me.* I would have chosen time with her over decorations any day of the year. Even Christmas Day.

For other young people, participating in rituals like putting up decorations together matters more to them. So they might feel betrayed or excluded by the same surprise that felt so welcoming to me. Thankfully, you don't have to wonder how to prepare for your kid at the holidays. Just ask! The holidays, the decorations, and the food present another opportunity for a pre-conversation that lets your emerging adult share what matters most to them while they're home.

three

LIFE STAGE MILESTONES

GRADUATING FROM

While not every kid will go to college, about 70 percent of all high school graduates attend a postsecondary institution. So chances are, your young adult will graduate at some point from a school, training program, or military boot camp. These are important milestones that mark a significant step in their journey. And graduation is *always* a reason to celebrate.

Celebration. This could be a home-cooked meal at home or an evening out at a favorite restaurant. Ask your graduate if there are significant adults or mentors they would like to invite.

Before asking, "What's next?," consider that college students often are already bombarded with that question. They've just finished a huge accomplishment, and people are already asking them what they're going to do next. As trusted adults, take time to reflect with them on the program they just graduated, and ask some of these questions instead:

- "What did you love most?"
- "What are you going to miss?"
- "How do you think you've changed?"
- "What's going to help you most as you look ahead?"

GRADUATING TO

When your kid graduates *from* a program, they also graduate *toward* whatever might be next for them. For some, they already have a job, more training, or graduate school lined up. For others, the search for what's next is just starting. No matter where your graduate stands, this is a time of opportunity that can feel both exciting and overwhelming.

It's entirely possible that this transition will be the most dramatic of any they've experienced so far. While college, military, a new roommate, or a first work experience were big jumps from high school, most young adults during these times still maintained a similar world with built-in accountability, like grades, assignments, orders, or defined roles.

When they graduate college, however, emerging adults now move out even further, potentially to new careers in new cities, with new communities, and new experiences. Familiar patterns of relationship and life management will change and emerging adults will likely experience at least some level of anxiety, loneliness, and disorientation. They'll need your support as they process this new transition that brings them closer to adulthood.

NAVIGATING FUTURE AND FAITH

—

CRITICAL ISSUES TO ANTICIPATE

NAVIGATE THE CRITICAL ISSUES

EVERY PHASE HAS NEW CHALLENGES. FOR EMERGING ADULTS, NEW FRONTIERS ASSOCIATED WITH FAITH, HEALTH, SEX, AND TECHNOLOGY CAN EITHER HELP OR HURT THEM. THESE FOUR TOPICS ARE IMPORTANT, NOT BECAUSE THEY CAN BE "DANGEROUS," BUT BECAUSE THEY BECOME EXPRESSIONS OF THE WAY EMERGING ADULTS SEE THEIR WORLD, THEMSELVES, AND THEIR RELATIONSHIP WITH GOD AND OTHERS.

THE TRUTH IS, YOUR KID IS OLD ENOUGH TO MAKE THEIR OWN DECISIONS ABOUT THESE TOPICS. MAKING DECISIONS FOR THEM MAY BE TEMPTING, BUT IT WILL ONLY HINDER THEIR GROWING-UP PROCESS.

YOUR ROLE IS TO BE A CONVERSATION PARTNER.

KEEP COMMUNICATION CHANNELS OPEN, **EVEN** IF YOU DISAGREE WITH THEM.

MAYBE EVEN **ESPECIALLY** WHEN YOU DISAGREE WITH THEM.

one

IMAGINE THE FUTURE

It's funny to think about imagining the end when your adult kid's life is just beginning. But as therapist Meg Jay reminds us, emerging adults are sometimes hindered by assuming they have until 30 to get their act together. In some ways, this is true. It may be several years before they step fully into adulthood. But the 18+ phase is still vitally important and often sets a trajectory for the rest of their lives.

Seventy percent of lifetime wage growth happens in the first 10 years of a career.

Fifty percent of Americans are married, living with, or dating their future partner by 30.

To help twenty-somethings better prepare for what is to come, Jay asks emerging adults how they envision their futures:

"What is it that you want?"
"Where would you like to be in five or ten years?"
"Do you want to get married?"
"Do you want to have kids?"
"What do you want your job to be?"

Using these early years to help clarify what they want will go a long way in helping your emerging adult set goals and move toward them.

two

AUTHENTIC FAITH

Attending church isn't always a priority to young adults. For years, research has pointed to a large percentage of high school graduates leaving the church after high school *and* a growing number of them failing to return in early adulthood.

Maybe that isn't the case for your kid. Awesome! But chances are their beliefs are still changing in some way, even if they're still attending church.

The truth is growth requires change. And part of developing a grown-up faith is allowing what you've always believed to be shaped, changed, or experienced in a new way. The goal isn't for them to live out *the beliefs given to them*, but to develop an authentic faith of their own.

For many young adults, post-high school is the first time they have to make decisions based on the beliefs they hold. It might be the first time they've encountered someone who has very different beliefs as them, but is just as devout. It's the first time they've had to really own their beliefs for themselves, rather than rely on the belief of other authority figures like parents, pastors, or youth pastors. As a result, emerging adults will need to question, test, and explore the way they express their faith before they make it their own. But testing isn't easy. This process can make them feel very vulnerable (and makes their parents anxious).

Remember, the spiritual investment you've made in them matters. Lots of research suggests that the greatest influence in a young person's life is mom and dad. The investment that you've made all those weeks leading up until now is important and doesn't disappear once your kid goes to college. Even if they don't talk about it, don't act like it, or don't agree *right now*, what you've taught them about life and faith is still *in* them.

But that doesn't mean your job is over!

One of the best indicators that your kid will live a life of authentic faith as an adult is if *you* live a life of authentic faith as an adult.

After studying the faith development of more than three thousand young people nationwide from Protestant, Roman Catholic, Jewish, and Mormon families, Christian Smith and his team concluded, "The best general rule of thumb that parents might use to reckon their children's most likely religious outcomes rests not on what we say, but in how we live ourselves: 'We'll get what we are.'"

Still . . .

Remember that their faith isn't your faith. Some parents and adults get worried, even frustrated, when young adults express their faith differently. Sure, sometimes those arguments center around issues like music, style of worship, or whether a *real* pastor can wear jeans. But sometimes there are deeper disagreements, too. You may find that your adult kid not only worships differently, but *believes* some different things than you that is reshaping their social, political, and ethical outlooks (which can certainly make holiday dinners more exciting).

And that is *good news.*

When young adults make changes in the way they express faith, this often indicates that they are making their faith their own and seeking to live it out. They're internalizing their faith. They may not be rejecting their past, only building on their past to develop a future faith.

But even if they disagree with you, they need to know that having doubts and questions does not mean that they are being unfaithful. In fact, it means that they have the courage and confidence to think more deeply about their own beliefs. It's all part of having a grown-up, mature faith.

It's helpful not only to share the successful faith stories in your life, but also those seasons when your faith really struggled. This normalizes their own experience and gives them permission to talk about the things that don't make sense, that trouble them, or that they doubt.

Remember that for your kid, faith and doubt have belief consequences, but also relational consequences. When a kid is doubting, questioning, or revising their faith, parents and pastors see this as an intellectual hurdle for them. Adults then give them books, more information, and sermons that defend the faith. The reality, however, is that most young adults worry less about the intellectual tension they feel, and more about the relational fallout they might experience if they don't believe what their parents, youth pastor, or church believes anymore. Your kid needs to know their relationship with you is solid, no matter what they believe. If they know that, they are more likely to invite you into their own faith journey.

Remember that their faith affects your faith. The reason that adults often become anxious about their kid's spiritual questioning and choices actually has less to do with their worry for their kids, and more about how they feel anxious about their own faith. Some say that both faith and doubt are contagious. For instance, if your son or daughter expresses doubts about God, it can evoke your own questions or resurrect old challenges that you have ignored. This can feel embarrassing, threatening, and disorienting. Avoid the temptation to run from these feelings. Just as your kid's faith is growing and developing, so is yours. This is your opportunity to learn and grow together.

THE OTHER END (OF THIS BOOK)

IT'S BEEN SAID THAT ONCE YOU BECOME A PARENT, YOU NEVER STOP BEING ONE. THIS INSIGHT MAY FEEL MOST REAL FOR PARENTS OF 18+ KIDS. WHILE EARLIER PARENTING PHASES HAVE AN AGE-DEFINED FINISH LINE, THE 18+ PHASE LAUNCHES US INTO CONTINUAL NEW BEGINNINGS AND REMINDS US THAT OUR PARENTING MORPHS AS OUR KIDS CHANGE. MAY OUR PARENTING NEVER BECOME A STATIC LABEL OR AUTOPILOT EXISTENCE. RATHER, IN THIS PHASE . . .

LET'S NEVER STOP DISCOVERING WHO OUR KIDS ARE AND LEARNING ABOUT WHO WE ARE. LET'S PRACTICE LETTING GO AND SEARCH FOR NEW WAYS OF CONNECTING. LET'S CUT THEM SOME SLACK AND ACCEPT GRACE FOR OUR OWN MISTAKES. LET'S REMEMBER THAT THERE'S NO KID LIKE YOURS AND THAT THERE'S NO BETTER PARENT FOR THEM THAN YOU.

WELCOME TO ONE OF THE MOST EXCITING CHAPTERS IN THE JOURNEY OF PARENTING BEYOND AGE 18!

ENDNOTES

1. Arnett, Emerging Adulthood.

2. This concept has been used by many, referencing the work by Erikson, Erik H. Identity and the Life Cycle. New York: W. W. Norton & Company, 1994.

3. https://nces.ed.gov/programs/digest/d16/ tables/dt16_105.20.asp?current=yes

4. Bureau of Labor Statistics. "America's Young Adults at 27: Labor Market Activity, Education, and Household Composition: Results from a Longitudinal Survey." BLS.gov, April 8, 2016. http://www.bls.gov/news.release/nlsyth.nr0.htm

5. Patte, Eileen, and Richard Fry. "How Millennials Compare with Their Grandparents." Pew Research Center, March 19, 2015. http://www.pewresearch.org/fact-tank/2015/03/19/ how-millennials-compare-with-their-grandparents/

6. Friedman, Stacey R., and Carol S. Weissbrod. "Work and Family Commitment and Decision-Making Status Among Emerging Adults." Sex Roles 53, no. 5 (September 2005): 317-25. doi:10.1007/s11199-005-6755-2

7. Barry, Carolyn M., Stephanie D. Madsen, and Alyssa DeGrace. "Growing Up with a Little Help from their Friends in Emerging Adulthood." In The Oxford Handbook of Emerging Adulthood, edited by Jeffrey Arnett. New York: Oxford University Press, 2015.

8. Smith, Christian, Kari Chrisoffersen, Hilary Davidson, and Patricia S. Herzog. Lost in Transition: The Dark Side of Emerging

Adulthood. New York: Oxford University Press, 2011.

9. Cohn, D'Vera, Jeffrey S. Passel, Wendy Wang, and Gretchen Livingston. "Barely Half of U.S. Adults Are Married - A Record Low." Pew Research Center, Deceber 14, 2011. http://www.pewsocialtrends. org/2011/12/14/barely-half-of-u-s-adults-are-married-a-record-low

10. Kay, Alan. "Distracting Ourselves to Death" (plenary address presented at the annual meeting of the Media Ecology Association, St. Louis, Mississippi, June 20, 2009).

11. Arnett, Jeffrey. "How Digital Natives Spend Their Time." OUPblog, March 21, 2015. http://blog.oup.com/2015/03/ digital-natives-emerging-adulthood-infographic/ see also Alloy, 2009, College Explorer Survey

12. Clydesdale, Tim. The First Year Out: Understanding American Teens After High School. Chicago: The University of Chicago Press, 2007, 15 and 40.

13. Arnett, Emerging Adulthood, 9.

14. Powell, Kara, Jake Mulder, and Brad Griffin. Growing Young: Six Essential Strategies to Help Young People Discover and Love Your Church. Grand Rapids: Baker Books, 2016.

15. https://www.urmc.rochester.edu/encyclopedia/content. aspx?ContentTypeID=1&ContentID=3051

16. Beck, Melinda. "Delayed development: 20-Somethings Blame the Brain." The Wall Street Journal, August 23, 2012. http:// www.wsj.com/articles/SB10000872396390443713704577601532 208760746; Trible, Hannah B. "Emerging Adulthood: Defining the Life Stage and its Developmental Tasks." Educational Specialist 2 (2015). http://commons.lib.jmu.edu/cgi/viewcontent. cgi?article=1007&context=edspec201019; Taber-Thomas, Bradley, and Koraly Perez-Edgar. "Emerging Adulthood Brain Development." In The Oxford Handbook of Emerging Adulthood, edited by Jeffrey Arnett. New York: Oxford University Press, 2015.